EVAN PLACEY

Evan Placey is a Canadian-British playwright who grew up in Toronto and now lives in London, England. His plays include *Mother of Him* (Courtyard Theatre; winner of the King's Cross Award for New Writing, RBC National Playwriting Competition, Canada, and the Samuel French Canadian Play Contest); *Banana Boys* (Hampstead Theatre); *Suicide(s) in Vegas* (Canadian tour; Centaur Theatre Award nomination); *Scarberia* (Forward Theatre Project/York Theatre Royal); *How Was It For You?* (Unicorn Theatre); *Holloway Jones* (Synergy Theatre Project/schools tour/Unicorn Theatre; winner of the Brian Way Award 2012 for Best Play for Young People; Writers' Guild Award nomination); *Girls Like That* (Synergy/Unicorn Theatre; first produced and commissioned by Birmingham Repertory Theatre, Theatre Royal Plymouth and West Yorkshire Playhouse; winner of the Writers' Guild Award for Best Play for Young Audiences); *Pronoun* (National Theatre Connections) and *Consensual* (National Youth Theatre in the West End). Work for radio includes *Mother of Him* (BBC Radio 3/Little Brother Productions).

Evan is a Creative Fellow and Senior Lecturer at the University of Southampton, and also teaches playwriting to young people for various theatres, and also in prisons.

Evan Placey

GIRLS LIKE THAT

NICK HERN BOOKS
London
www.nickhernbooks.co.uk

A Nick Hern Book

Girls Like That first published in Great Britain as a paperback original in 2013 by Nick Hern Books Limited, The Glasshouse, 49a Goldhawk Road, London W12 8QP, in association with Birmingham Repertory Theatre, Theatre Royal Plymouth and West Yorkshire Playhouse

Reprinted 2014, 2015, 2016

Girls Like That copyright © 2013 Evan Placey

Evan Placey has asserted his right to be identified as the author of this work

Cover photograph by Matthew Hargraves
Image design by John McAreavy for West Yorkshire Playhouse
Cover design by Ned Hoste, 2H

Typeset by Nick Hern Books, London

Printed and bound in Great Britain by CPI Books (UK) Ltd

A CIP catalogue record for this book is available from the British Library

ISBN 978 1 84842 353 4

Girls Like That was commissioned by Birmingham Repertory Theatre, Theatre Royal Plymouth and West Yorkshire Playhouse.

The play was first performed by The Young REP as part of The Young Rep Festival at The Old Rep Theatre, Birmingham, on 12 July 2013; the West Yorkshire Playhouse Youth Theatre at the Courtyard Theatre, West Yorkshire Playhouse, on 18 July 2013; and by the Theatre Royal Plymouth Young Company at the Theatre Royal Plymouth, on 14 August 2013.

The three companies were as follows:

BIRMINGHAM REPERTORY THEATRE

Kimberley Atkiss
Dayna Batman
Victoria Bowes
Anushka Chakravarti
Heather Fantham
Rebekka Ford
Sophie Lines
Anna Piper
Jordan Perkins
Nathan Queeley-Dennis
Roisin Richardson
Kesia Schofield
Aurora Tanda
Melissa Uppal

Director	Daniel Tyler
Festival Designer	Oliver Shapley
Festival Stage Manager	Amber Curtis
Festival Production Manager	Tomas Wright
Festival Costumes by	Birmingham Repertory Theatre
Festival Lighting by	The Old Rep Theatre
Festival Technician	Anthony Aston
Young REP Company Support	Emma Ledsam

6

WEST YORKSHIRE PLAYHOUSE

Daisy Addison
Emily Anderson-Wallace
Lydia Crosland
Megan Dawson
Jessica Finlay
Mabel Goulden
Zoe Hamilton
Catherine Hawthorn
Edward House
Bethan Johnson
Hannah Kilcoyne
Hal Lockwood
Laura Marsden
Alistair McKenzie
Holly Pennington
Harri Pitches
Uma Ramachadran
Alice Rayner
Natasha Brotherdale Smith
Lizzie Turner

Director	Gemma Woffinden
Set Designer	Chris Cully
YP Design	Dylon Rawnsley
& Construction Assistants	& Abena Weston
Costume Designer	Victoria Marzetti
YP Costume Design Assistants	Samantha Metcalfe
	& Ella Robbins
Lighting Designer	Paul Lovett
YP Lighting Design Assistants	Sam Gosling & Ben Lander
Sound Designer	Ian Robert Trollope
YP Sound Design Assistant	Joe Bellwood
Movement Director	Sophie Hudson
Fight Director	Gavin Harding
Assistant to the Director	Amy Oddy
Production Manager	Suzi Cubbage
YP Production Manager	Loren Rayner
Stage Manager	Julie Issott
YP Stage Manager	Rachel Robertson

Special thanks to: Andrew Potterton for original music, Air Transport
Auxiliary Museum, Maidenhead Carphone Warehouse

THEATRE ROYAL PLYMOUTH YOUNG COMPANY

Alice Cadmore
Senga Clarke-Côté
Elizabeth Edwards
Alisha Lee
Libby Long
Sinead Millar
Lorrine Penwarden
Rosie Stevenson
Abigail Summers
Amy Wallace
Zoe Walton
Talia Winn
Simon Hill
Danny Laine
William Lewis
JJ McColl
Lewis Peek

Director	Beth Shouler
Assistant Director	Liam Salmon
Designer	Fiona Evans
Assistant Designer	Nina Raines
Producer	Jane Pawson
Production Manager	Nick Soper
Lighting Designer	John Perkis
Sound Designer	Holly Harbottle
Theatre Technician	Matt Hoyle
Stage Manager	Brooke Tippett
Deputy Stage Manager	Natasha Whitley*
Assistant Stage Manager	Thomas Michaels*

* Young Company Members

Acknowledgements

This play was a team effort, involving the dedication and support of many people. Thank you to:

Everyone at Birmingham Rep, West Yorkshire Playhouse, and Theatre Royal Plymouth, and especially: Gemma Woffinden, Beth Shouler, Daniel Tyler, Alex Chisholm, Jessica Farmer, Victoria Allen, Jane Pawson, David Prescott, Tessa Walker, and Caroline Jester.

Everyone at the Unicorn Theatre and Synergy Theatre, especially Esther Baker, for bringing renewed life and creativity to the play.

The many young people – too many to name here – who shared with me their insights and ideas; thank you all for your honesty.

Tanya Tillett, for talking sense into me every once in a while.

Mom, Dad, Lindsay and Jay, for your constant support.

Daniel, for believing in me and loving me even when I act like a teenager.

E.P.

For Zoey, and the woman she grows up to be

Characters

GIRLS, *up to nineteen of them, division of lines up to the company*
GIRL IN FLAPPER DRESS
GIRL WITH AVIATOR HELMET AND GOGGLES
GIRL WITH FLOWERS IN HER HAIR
GIRL WITH SHOULDER PADS
SCARLETT

A Note on Stage Directions and Punctuation

Change is a change in time. It should be quite quick. It might be indicated by a change in light, or a sound, or in the actors changing position on stage or all of these or none of these.

An ellipsis (…) is a trailing off/loss of words/search for words. It is not a cut-off.

A dash (–) is a cut-off. Sometimes by one's own thought being intercepted by another thought. These are not pauses or beats.

A lack of punctuation means the next line comes right in.

This text went to press before the end of rehearsals and so may differ slightly from the play as performed.

The GIRLS *stand at the front of the stage facing the audience.*

GIRLS   Slut

Skank

Sket

Ho

Prossie

Whore

Slag

Tart

Tramp

Hussy

Floozie

Ho-bag

Slapper

You deserve everything coming to you

Skanky Scarlett

Slutty Scarlett

Scarlett the Harlot

Slut

Slut

Slut

Slut

Slut

Slut

Slut

Slut.

Beat.

Music. 'Run the World (Girls)' by Beyoncé. The GIRLS *put on headphones. The* GIRLS *sing along and dance – a routine they've clearly practised before. The music suddenly stops. The* GIRLS *take off their headphones. Five years old.*

When Scarlett arrives her hair is in these two messy pigtail braids, and she has Ribena stained around her mouth.

We are five years old. I am by the sandbox making a princess castle that more accurately resembles a large horse's shit.

I am by the water tub – I like the way the water feels when it runs through the little blonde hairs on my wrist.

I'm on the carpet picking my nose still unsure why this lady who looks like Nanny McPhee is to replace my mother when another girl makes a beeline straight for me. She sits right next to me, our knees touching. And I know I am special. I have been chosen.

My mother told me not to pick my nose in public.

My mother told me not to bite my nails.

My mother told me not to be so loud.

What my mother told me means nothing on the first day of reception at St Helen's School for Girls.

Clearly my mother is an idiot. I have been duped. Because the girl picking her nose with the chewed-down pinky is now sitting next to the most popular girl in class. I will never listen to my mother again.

St Helen's is a special school. I know this because my mother told me so.

St Helen's is a special school because it only accepts twenty five-year-olds each year, selected for our gifted academic ability and creative potential to think outside the box, demonstrated through a test with questions like 'Sophie has a car with only one working door. She has five friends who each take forty-five seconds to enter through the door and get in their seat. How many of them will be seated ninety seconds after Sophie unlocks the door?'

All of them. The car is a convertible.

St Helen's is special because me and these twenty girls

These twenty girls and I will progress through the next seven years of primary together, always the same classmates, the same twenty girls, forging long-lasting friendships, and bonds of camaraderie and sisterhood. My mother would call this special. I would call this hell.

Twenty girls from different parts of the city, different backgrounds, who might not otherwise have ever crossed paths.

If only.

But here at St Helen's, in this grey classroom we will become a family. A Benetton ad. In prison.

I live on a farm. We have chickens. And every time we get some new hens, it starts again – it lasts no more than five minutes, but they battle it out, to determine the pecking order. They jump on each other's backs, push the other with their chests, rip feathers out of each other with their beaks. They go until it's clear who goes where in the hierarchy. My brother, he's older, he's seven, he cries whenever this happens, tries to pull them apart, the referee. But I am a five-year-old girl. I stand back and watch. I understand.

At St Helen's we are civilised little girls. We humans are much more clever than hens. We do not need to fight. We know it, the pecking order.

Who's at the top

Who's in the middle

Who's at the bottom

Just as every girl at every other school in the city knows it

Is sitting in their own classroom, eyeing up the others

Smelling the others

Positioning themselves in the order that will determine the rest of their lives.

I am in the middle. A comfortable place to be. I'd recommend to any five-year-old that this is the wisest place to be.

Definitely.

Scarlett is at the bottom. Full stop.

Beat.

I join the others on the carpet for circle time. I don't know if it's for a game or maybe we just do it – instinctively just reach out to our neighbours, interlock fingers – but we're all holding hands.

An unspoken pact sealed.

These girls are my friends. My mother told me these girls are my friends for life.

And she's got chocolate on her fingers from breakfast.

And she's got bits of Play-Doh under her fingernails.

And her hands are wet from the water tub.

But we let it pass. It's the first day. And we're happy to be here. Twenty special girls.

Twenty little girls holding hands.

Change. Present.

We're in history when it comes.

Miss is droning on, highlighting keywords on the board, and every time she raises her arm to write you can like see her bingo wings through the opening of her sleeve. Like someone should really tell her it's illegal for fifty-year-olds to wear short sleeves. Maybe I'll like write her a note. Anonymously of course. But as a courtesy like.

I am texting a boy. There are no boys in history.

Secondary school is mixed, so we can see the male species in the corridors and stuff, make sure we don't all turn out to be lesbians, but otherwise it's still just the girls. But other girls too. Three schools feed into St Margaret's. And so it's nice, like really honestly nice to still have all my primary-school friends with me. The St Helen's girls.

The St Helen's girls. Or the Satan Hell girls as some of the others call us. As a joke y'know.

It's nice to have girls that really know me, that remember in year three when I won the singing competition with my rendition of 'Since U Been Gone'.

It's nice to have girls that remember our school trip in year five when the bus broke down and we had a slumber party on the bus.

Girls who remember the swimming relay when I came first

Girls who remember the music teacher's meltdown

Girls who remember the time I laughed so hard I peed a bit

Girls who remember when my period went on the cafeteria bench and I refused to get up

Girls who remember that my mum had an affair with the maths teacher

Girls who remember that I was the only one in the year not invited to the end-of-year pool party

Girls who remember when I was in the toilet and missed my entrance in the school play

Girls who remember when I put my tampon in cord-end first and had to go to hospital

Girls who remember when I asked Nurse Nancy if a clitoris was a kind of dinosaur

Girls who never forget.

Beat.

Us girls are sitting in history not listening to Miss's McMuffin-breath ramble on about voting or suffering jets or something when it comes.

Buzz

Click

Pop

Flash

A text

An email

A message

A tweet

And the classroom is brighter as phones come alight

It's not like I was the only one checking

Everyone got it, not just me so it's not like

Which is why, when I, like it wouldn't have changed anything

A photo of Scarlett. Naked.

Beat.

Buzz

Click

Pop

Flash

O-M-G

What a little slut

What a little skank

When the chickens start attacking each other, like really going for it, they can draw blood, and that's when, that's when you need to be really careful. Because if they see blood, the other chickens, they can turn into murderers. They'll keep pecking until there's more blood and more. So you have to get this antiseptic spray that sprays purple, so the chickens don't notice the red blood. Or else they'll peck the chicken to death. I don't know why. But I think it's maybe cos a vulnerable chicken is putting the whole flock at risk. Or something.

And it's funny

And it's kind of sexy

And it's ugly

And so I

And so I

And so I

DELETE.

Beat.

And it's over.

Beat.

Except I don't.

Because someone else will

Someone else will definitely anyway

So I

Forward

Tweet

Poke

Send

Forward

Tweet

Poke

Send

Buzz

Click

Pop

Flash.

And it's not like…

I didn't send the photo out in the first place

If a photo's taken and no one's there to see it, was it really taken? I mean didn't Plato or someone say that?

And there's a rumour that the school internet crashes from all the activity.

There's a rumour that makes no sense whatsoever since obviously no one's allowed to use the school internet on their phones and they're using 3G

What is definitely true is that within three minutes of
receiving the photo in the middle of Miss saying
something about a woman who got tied up to
Parliament – some crazy *Fifty Shades* shit or something
– everyone in the school has acquired the photo.

Or maybe it's not to do with protecting the flock at all.
Maybe it's just that chickens are horrible murderous
bitches. You'd have to ask a chicken farmer really.

Music. 'Wings' by Little Mix. GIRLS *put their
headphones on. Again they sing along and do a dance
to it – this time leading it though is a* GIRL IN
FLAPPER DRESS. *Her appearance and manner are
at odds with the contemporary song, but she knows all
the words and the dance.*

The song suddenly stops. The GIRLS *keep their
headphones on, face the back/away.*

GIRL IN FLAPPER DRESS

The invitation reads: 'Mrs Plunkett Greene, Miss
Ponsonby, Mr Edward Gathorne-Hardy and Mr Brian
Howard request the pleasure of my company at St
George's Swimming Baths, Buckingham Palace Road,
11 o'clock p.m. on Friday, 12th of July, 1928. Please
wear a bathing suit and bring a bath towel and a bottle.
Each guest is required to show his invitation on arrival.'

The colours of the other girls' suits are dazzling. Some
of them change suits two or three times throughout the
evening. I've only brought the one. But I don't mind.

I flirt with the trumpet player from the Negro band. I
flirt with one of the cocktail mixers, who's also wearing
a bathing costume. I even flirt with the rubber horses
that float above the water. This is the single-most
greatest night in my life thus far. I shall never forget it.

And then I see him. Out of place in his full suit
amongst the semi-naked bodies. Eyes darting
nervously. Until he spots what he's looking for: me.

'I'm taking you home right now.'

And one of the other girls wanders over. 'I didn't know you had a fella.'

'I don't. He's my brother.'

'Cute. I hope he's brought a bathing costume.'

'I haven't,' he interjects. He doesn't like being spoken about in the third person.

'Well then I guess you'll have to go nude. You won't be the first.' And she laughs.

My clothes are somewhere inside. So my brother drapes his jacket around my bare arms. 'We can get them tomorrow.'

'She's only just got here. She hasn't even swum yet.'

And then he turns on her. 'I'm not talking to you.'

But the girl's not listening, or doesn't care. 'Do you have a light,' she wants to know. A cigarette dangling from her lips.

I want to avoid this. But a Negro saxophonist is riffing and some girls are splashing in the water and some girls are spilling their Martini glasses and he can't contain himself.

'No. And I don't think it's very ladylike to be smoking in public.'

And this time she hears him loud and clear. She smiles. She can't tell if he's flirting or challenging her. She doesn't care either way. 'Oh. And why is that?'

And now I'm suddenly ready to go. I don't want to swim. I just want to leave. And why doesn't the band play louder? Why have they gone quiet just at the moment my brother says:

'Because people will mistake you for an ordinary whore.'

Play goddamit, why won't the band just play! And everyone is looking over. Everyone who a moment ago I was dancing with and drinking with are now looking over at my eighteen-year-old brother.

And then the music starts up again. Only it's not the band. It's the people. And they're not singing, they're laughing. My brother has underestimated his audience. Because if he'd looked around he'd have noticed girls all over the pool shamelessly smoking.

And the girl, she says: 'Shall I take that as a no then? You don't have a light?'

And the girls laugh even harder. And even I, I can't help it, and I start laughing too. I'm laughing so hard that I don't even see it coming.

Slap.

'If you want to act like a slut I'll treat you like one.'

My cheek is throbbing but the effort to touch it feels too much. My face is wet and I don't know whether it's tears or if someone has splashed from the pool. So I stand there clutching the inside pockets of my brother's jacket. And I wish I'd never come out tonight. I wish I'd just stayed home like a girl should. I'm sorry, I'm sorry, I'm sorry.

'You think our mother fought for your rights so you could behave like this?'

And as I'm leaving, my bare feet on the concrete – I feel something in my hand. In the pocket. Matches.

And I don't think about what I'm doing. My body takes on a life of its own and I've turned back. Everyone still watching. I strike a match.

Fizz. Pop.

And I light her cigarette.

And it feels like the best thing I've ever done in my life.

And my brother just looks at me. A look that says I won't forget this. A look that says just wait until we get home. And I know that I don't have a choice.

I throw off his jacket. And dive into the pool.

She exits. The GIRLS *take off their headphones and turn around.*

GIRLS   Scarlett has a mole on the top of her left breast. Well my left, her right. And it, or actually maybe it's her left too, cos the camera does it in reverse, right? Does it? I'm confused.

She probably wants to get that checked out. Check it's not Aids or something.

Probably should get that mole removed. Cos you never know. And boys don't like markings. Unless they're one of those Goth types who likes girls with tattoos and piercings – boys like girls with smooth skin.

I saw a movie once where this girl had a piercing in her fanny.

On closer inspection, I decide it's actually a freckle. When I enlarge it on my screen, zoom in, you can see it's a freckle.

And her nipples are large, like really – like that's not normal is it?

And the way she's positioned, there's like this line on her stomach, this line of blubber on her belly. I didn't know she was fat until now. But she is. She's fat.

Fat slut

And she hasn't even bothered to, I mean it's a jungle, like if you're going to, at least wax beforehand, it's like a guinea pig died.

Looks pretty normal to me.

It's a dead guinea pig.

And I feel good because she's a hairy ape

And I feel good because my breasts are bigger than hers

And I feel good because my breasts are smaller than her abnormally large ones

And I feel good because her arms are short

And I feel good because her shoulders are bony

And I feel good because her belly button is an outie

And I feel good because her nail polish is chipped

And I feel good because she has a mole on her right or left breast

And I feel good because she's a slut and not even that pretty.

There are rumours that Scarlett gave Russell a BJ in the toilets after school last week. I didn't believe it at the time, but this proves it. This is like... rock-hard evidence.

I believed it all along. With girls like that you can just tell.

And the thing with rumours, yeah, is that they wouldn't be rumours if there weren't at least some truth in them. Like they wouldn't have come about in the first place if they weren't at least say seventy percent true. So like maybe it wasn't in the toilets, or maybe it wasn't after school – that's the thirty percent that might be wrong, but she definitely gave him a blowjob. That's what matters.

Miss is still talking about *feminism* and the word reminds me of *femidom* like Nurse Nancy told us about so I start laughing, and when she asks me why I'm laughing I tell her I have a disability.

I secretly take a photo of Miss, and while she's blubbering on about voting I have put her face on

Scarlett's naked body. My mum once got detention for making a cartoon drawing of one of her teachers. But I'm not worried, my phone is password protected.

At lunch the corridor is buzzing, is popping, and boys are smirking. The first moments of lunch when classes spill out and the sexes come tumbling together in the corridor is a bit like when I used to volunteer at the dogs' home. The dogs are all anxious to come out of their cages, can't sit still, but as soon as you open the doors, most of 'em barely come out at first. Tentative. Backs against the cage, against the lockers, but pretty soon they get over that and everybody's humping and smelling each other's arses.

Girls flick immaculate hair, boys steal furtive glances while pretending to talk to their friends, holding tight to the straps of their rucksacks as if they're cords of a bomb and they might combust.

A boy says: 'Guess I know what I'm doing tonight.'

Another laughs and says: 'Wank bank.'

'Slut.'

'Whore.'

But that's not the boys. That's what's weirdest, while the girls are zooming, highlighting, cutting, pasting, analysing, comparing thoughts and insights into Scarlett, the boys are… well they're not doing much of anything. Just smirking. Like fucking buffoons. Like they don't get it. Like they… y'know?

And then one of them finally speaks.

'I'd tap it.' Tyler. That's what he says.

Like even though she's a, and she's just…

'I don't think you should be looking at that.' A boy says this. Jay.

Maybe he fancies Scarlett, or maybe he's drunk, or maybe he's looking for a fight.

But Jay's not the fighting type. He's not a boy like that. He's just a boy who happens to be at his locker.

'You what?' It's Tyler.

'You what? Do you got a little hard-on for her do you? Want the photo all to yourself?'

'No. That's not. I haven't seen it actually.'

Like he's above it or something. Though probably he's lying. Everyone's seen it.

And Tyler laughs. 'Well here mate. Share and share alike.' And Tyler passes the phone to him.

But Jay averts his gaze. 'No. Thanks.'

'You what?'

'It's none of my…' His resolve's fading. 'I just don't think…'

'You gay or something?' Some other boy has piped up.

'Bet you are. That's why your parents named you Jay. Cos it rhymes with gay.'

Logic doesn't really matter at this point.

It doesn't matter that Jay has a girlfriend which even douchebag Tyler knows.

It also doesn't matter that Jay plays football with them and scored a winning shot last week and that they put him on their shoulders.

What matters is Jay has temporarily set everything off-balance. He has told them there is no Santa Claus. He has questioned gravity. The cosmos need to be realigned.

'Maybe if it was a photo of you Tyler, then he'd look.'

'Oh, is that it gay Jay? Are you saving your eyes for my – '

And before he can finish with some awful metaphor for his genitals, Jay does it. He looks at the photo. And I'm a bit angry at how easily he gives in. How easily he sighs and looks.

'I knew it. You totally have a woody for her. You'd tap it right?'

And he: 'Yeah. I'd tap it.' And even from where I'm standing I can hear the monotone. He'd make a terrible actor. Jay goes. And I wait for the boys to talk about Jay, to talk about what's just happened. But they don't. It's like. It's like it didn't happen.

Snog marry kill. Harry, Niall, Zayn.

And then the corridor goes silent, like proper.

And it reminds me of the time I met Lady Gaga. Well not really met, but you know what I mean. And I had this CD cover of Gaga's face for her to sign, and she's there like two feet in front of me, and it's her, it's definitely her from the cover, but just less... I dunno. Like she was still as hot and as cool as the her on the cover, but just a bit... normal.
And there's Scarlett looking up at me from my phone screen, and there she is two feet away from me, and the two images, the two Scarletts... they're just different is all. One's just a bit more... *human*. Though I'm not totally sure which one.

And another thing about boys is they don't have any social awareness. Like they are completely socially unaware. They do not have what my mother would call *tact*. Because us girls don't say anything. Like obviously we would never say anything to her face. Cos that would just be... outrageous.

That would be completely rude.

And so we say nothing.

And Scarlett says: 'Hey.'

And it's kind of to all of us and none of us.

'Hey.'

But we don't say anything. Cos we're not like the boys.

No.

Beat.

We just pretend she's not there.

Personally, I don't think she was actually talking to me.

Nor me.

Personally, I don't think she was talking to anyone. It was more of a 'hey'. More like a sound really.

The problem with girls like that is they ruin it for everyone.

The problem with girls like that is they give all girls a bad name.

The problem with girls like that is that their reputation is contagious. And if you hang around girls like that, it's not necessarily that you'll start behaving like she does – we are intelligent young women, we have minds of our own – but people will think you do. And that's worse really.

We did a history class on the Holocaust, and learned about bystanders, who watched, stood by and even though they weren't performing the acts themselves, but just like being there, doing nothing, it's like… they're condoning it. And this is a bit like that. Like if I hang out with her, I'm approving of her behaviour.

And it wasn't planned, but we all just turn away, like turn our backs. Like a wave. All the St Helen's girls just silently turning. And I feel... part of something, y'know. I feel deeply connected to these girls I grew up with. And that's really nice.

These girls will be my friends for life.

And I'm gutted I didn't film it. Because it looked really beautiful. Balletic almost. It felt beautiful.

And my locker's open, so even though my back – through the mirror I can see what's happening. And Scarlett just stands there looking at us all. Willing our backs to move with her eyes or something like a witch.

And then she turns and looks to Russell.

Muscle Russell.

Tussled-hair Russell.

Lusty Russy.

Snog marry kill. Bed-head Russell. Football Russell. And dining-hall-eating Russell.

And that look, before he even says anything, confirms for me the rumours.

And I can't for sure say what her look was – as I can only see the back of her head. Pleading? Flirting? Accusing?

But he says: 'Again? I'm a bit worn out Scarlett.'

The boys laugh, some of them high-five.

I've never really understood the high-five. When I was twelve I tried it out, started high-fiving my best friend every time I saw her or I made a joke. But it just never really took off.

Boys can be such dicks.

Russell can do so much better. Hope he didn't catch an STI or something.

And as she slinks away, I feel really sorry for her. We all do I think. Maybe it's not all her fault. Maybe if her mother had just taught her better.

Change. Eight years old.

We are twenty girls squished into a teeny changing room at the local pool.

Arms touching arms. Legs touching legs.

I wish someone would move over.

I think they purposely make the changing rooms tiny and dirty and smelly so that people will not come to the local pool. I am fairly certain this is a conspiracy put in place by the moustache-lady who always yells at us for swimming in the wrong lane.

We are eight years old.

It is someone's birthday party and we are all there. That's the kind of close friends we are.

We are all there because the four mothers of the four girls who were not invited spoke to the mother of the girl who did the inviting. It wasn't me, I'm invited to everything on account of my mother being a local councillor.

About fifty percent of the girls wear one-pieces. Fifty percent wear bikinis.

Two-pieces, not bikinis.

And I change in the corner so no one can really see me.

I change in the middle, the other girls' bodies as a shield.

I change wherever cos comparatively I'm definitely one of the skinnier ones.

For a moment I'm worried I'll grow up to be fat.

For a moment I'm worried I'll grow up and become a lesbian.

For a moment I'm worried I'll grow up to be a cat lady who lives by herself.

For a moment I'm worried I'll never be pretty enough to get a boyfriend.

But then we're in the pre-showers and the water is freezing and we all scream and we forget.

Someone is not talking to Scarlett, and Scarlett is not talking to someone else, and someone else is not talking to someone else and I'm not sure what happened but I have to take someone's side so I take someone else's side, and we all reshuffle so someone else doesn't have to be near Scarlett. And someone, maybe me, has to act as messenger passing messages between the two.

And then we go swimming. Twenty squealing floral-printed bodies cannonballing into the water.

We count how long we can hold our breath.

We are mermaids.

Scarlett has brought Swimming Barbie who comes with waterproof make-up and we forgive Scarlett and the fight whatever it was about is forgotten.

And one of us pretends to be Ken asking Barbie out on a date, and we take turns to see who can think of the bestest line.

'Hey Barbie, wanna go for a ride in my convertible?'

'Hey Barbie, you've got to be the prettiest girl I ever did see. If you don't go out with me, I will kill myself.'

'Hey Barbie I want to kiss you with tongues.'

Ew.

Gross.

'Hey Barbie'

And Ken always has an American accent. We've never heard Ken speak before but decide he's such a hunk that he must be from California.

We do these somersault things over the rings that divide the lanes and moustache-lady yells at us. So we take turns secretly touching the rings, sitting on the rings when she's not looking, while the other girls distract her. Girls got to stick together right?

And she can't catch us, can't stop us. Because we are twenty and she is one. And we are only eight and she is more than that and still we are smarter.

Full up on pizza and cake and fizzy pop we run to the park next door and lie down damp in the grass.

We put our heads on each other's bellies so we're all connected. My head on her belly.

My head on hers.

Hers on hers.

And hers on hers.

And hers on hers.

Like a giant zigzagging water snake.

And we close our eyes to the flashing sun and listen to each girl's belly breath.

In. Out. In. Out.

And it is quiet.

Beat.

And then someone laughs, her belly vibrating into some other girl's wet hair.

So she in turn starts laughing

And then she in turn

And then she in turn

And soon there are twenty chuckling bellies, heads bouncing up and down, and still we keep our eyes closed.

And we laugh for what feels like hours.

We are in love with swimming, and summer, and each other, and Ken.

We are Barbie. We are mermaids. We are indestructible.

Change. Present.

After school Scarlett is nowhere to be seen.

Scarlett the Harlot.

Like no one has seen her since lunch.

If I were her I would totally kill myself. Talk about embarrassing. I just couldn't, y'know?

And I'm a bit worried.

We're all a bit worried. Because you hear stories and stuff. And it's just a stupid picture. She wouldn't do something stupid...

'We should call her,' someone says. Someone. Maybe me. Or one of the other – it doesn't really matter. What matters is we call her. All of us huddled around the phone on speaker.

...

'Hello?'

Scarlett?

'Hello?'

Yeah, Scarlett?

'Gotchya! You've reached Scarlett's VM. You know what to do. And if you don't I can't help you.'

She's not there, and we're worried, naturally, so we leave a message.

Scarlett, hi, this is a message for Scarlett Smith. This is *Playboy* magazine. We uh… (*Lowers voice.*) We uh loved your pics and would love for you to pose for us. So um… (*Laughs.*)

We hang up. We call again. We hang up. We call again. We hang up. We call again. We hang up. We call again. We call again. We call again. We call again. We call again.

This is um *Playboy* magazine

This is um *Penthouse* magazine

This is um *Nuts* magazine

This is um *Loaded* magazine

This is um *Zoo* magazine

This is um *FHM* magazine

This is um *New Statesman* magazine.

That's a political magazine you moron.

Sorry. Wrong number.
What? I saw my dad read it once.

We hang up. We call again. We hang up. We call again. We hang up. We call again. We call again. We call again. We call again. We go home.

En route I buy a *Closer* magazine.

En route I buy a *Heat* magazine.

En route I buy an *OK!* and a *Now* and a *HELLO!* because you get all three now in one package which is quite a good deal actually.

Kim Kardashian has gained a stone and has cellulite which is a shame because she was doing so well on her post-kid diet and now she looks disgusting.

And Cheryl Cole has lost a stone and her bingo wings and got a flat stomach and has the ideal body so Ashley Cole will be really jealous.

And Nicki Minaj is looking unhealthily skinny and an insider friend is worried about her.

And Drake is now single, and so is Taylor Lautner and so is Conor Maynard, they're all looking for a girl who knows how to have fun and doesn't take herself too seriously.

Kill marry snog. Drake, Lautner, Maynard.

Anyway you can't believe everything you read. Those magazines aren't always realistic. They probably all have girlfriends.

At home someone sends me the Scarlett photo. You're a bit behind the times my friend. As if I don't already have it. I look at it again anyway.

I look at it again.

I look at it again.

I read the comments people have posted on her Facebook page.

I look at it again.

My mother asks me what I'm looking at.

I tell her 'nothing'.

I tell her 'homework'.

I don't tell her anything.

She doesn't actually want to know the answer.

She's marking year eleven essays.

She's making a PowerPoint.

She's on the phone whinging about the bitch from work who stole her promotion.

She's telling my father about the girl from work who's going on maternity at what is a most inconvenient time for the company.

She's telling Grandma about the girl from the office who has to leave at three o'clock every day to pick up her kids, talk about a lack of commitment.

She's telling me about the slutty girl whose skirt was so short you could almost see the brand of her knickers.

She's telling no one in particular about how she got ID'd at Sainsbury's buying wine thank you very much.

She never actually asks.

She isn't home.

Buzz

Click

Pop

Flash

And a new photo has come through.

Someone else who is behind the times.

Except this time it's not Scarlett.

It's a different photo.

Russell. Completely naked.

*Music. 'California Gurls' by Katy Perry. Again the
girls put on headphones, sing along and do a dance.
This time the dance is led by a* GIRL WITH AVIATOR
HELMET AND GOGGLES.

The music suddenly stops. The GIRLS *face away with
their headphones.*

GIRL WITH AVIATOR HELMET AND GOGGLES
Let me give you some advice. Don't drink tea before
ya fly. I tell ya I couldn't *live* without me mornin' tea,
but nothing worse than bein' seven thousand feet in the
air, clouds everywhere, no navigation equipment or
radio aids and thinkin' I don't know how much longer
'fore I go in me knickers.

I try to tell this to the man who I've been assigned for
the day drinkin' a steamin' hot cup. It's February 1945.
Just another mornin' like any other at the Airport
Transport Auxillary – only today it's a Hudson I gotta
deliver for maintenance, which means there's gotta be
two of us. Me and this lad. And I'm tryin t' tell him,
give 'em some advice so I don't gotta be worried about
him needin' to wee up in the air, but he's havin' none of
it. Don't want t' hear it. Don't want t' hear none of it.

Don't even want t' be flyin with me. He's not takin'
orders from a lass.

Starts mumblin' 'bout what's the world coming to.
World at war, Britain bein' bombed, and t' top it all off
we got some lass flyin' planes. As though I'm the only
one. As though of the six hundred 'n' fifty ATA pilots,
a hundred 'n' sixty-four aren't women.

But he's insistin' he take charge. He's insistin'
otherwise this plane's goin' nowhere. And I can see
he's a stubborn so and so, so sometimes you gotta take
the higher ground, sometimes you gotta sit back and
say okay, you got a willy – you know best. Sometimes
when he's inspectin' the plane you gotta slip a laxative
into his tea.

It's about an hour later, I'm ready to go, but he's not feelin' so good, so they get some other pilot – and let's say he's much more amenable. As we're getting' into the plane I see the lad again, face ashen. So I tell him: 'Shoulda listened to my advice. Told you not to drink before ya fly.'

She exits. The GIRLS *take off their headphones, turn back to face us.*

GIRLS   Russell's body is what you would expect.

He goes to the gym.

He plays rugby.

It's as I imagined. That's not to say I spend my days picturing Russell naked, but if I did, that's what he would like look – like he does.

And the boys' nickname for him – Big Mac – well let's just say it's now clear it has nothing to do with his love of fast food.

And let's just say that when people said he was a bit ginger and I said no he's definitely blond – that I was right, thank God.

He should work in Hollister or something.

What is almost one hundred percent certain is that it was Scarlett who put the photo online. A likely hypothesis is that she did this as an act of revenge. What is less clear-cut is the motive for revenge which can be narrowed down to one of two possibilities: one – it was Russell who sent round the photo of her naked. Whether or not it actually was I can neither confirm nor deny, nor is it actually relevant, what's important is she believes it to be the case. Two – as revenge for embarrassing her in the corridor yesterday in front of everyone. What I can say for definite is that the photo of Russell has made its way round the entire school.

We should know this because girls are laughing. And boys are yelling 'man-whore' down the corridor. And Russell is standing alone by his locker with his head down.

Beat.

Except this is not what is happening. This is not how we know.

We know because one girl is heard stating she has changed her mind and she wants to marry Russell instead of snog him and is it too late to change?

We know this because a boy is heard saying: 'He's a legend, dude.'

We know this because Russell's friends are high-fiving him and acting like it is any other day.

The thing, yeah, and I'm sorry to have to be the one to say this, is that Scarlett, well she's obviously even dumber than she acts.

She obviously doesn't get it's fine for boys to be, you know.

They're supposed to be, right? Like it's part of their DNA, part of their puberty... blue balls or something. Wait. Is that right?

It is nature. It's not just chickens and cocks. I was watching the BBC and like even elephants, right, like there'll be like twelve female elephants, and one male for like all those women. The women will only have sex with the one male their whole life, but the male, well you do the math.

It's how it's meant to be. If you don't believe me ask David Attenborough.

Like my brother says: if a key can open lots of locks, it's a really good key. Like a master key. But if a lock can be opened by lots of keys then it's a really shit lock. Do you see?

And this is what Scarlett has failed to understand. Maybe her mother didn't teach her.

Boys will be boys.

Boys like Russell, a boy like that can't help himself.

A boy like that has to try before he buys.

One of the GIRLS *quotes the first four lines of 'A Boy Like That' from* West Side Story.

Actually, those are just the lyrics from *West Side Story*

Yeah, but. Well maybe. I was Anita on account of their being no Puerto Ricans at the school and my being a quarter Indian.

There's a group of boys looking at the photo, but it's weird. Cos like they're looking at it, but not. Like each of them keep flicking their eyes away from the screen, like if they look at it too long their eyes will burn.

Like they're afraid.

Like they're scared of being caught looking at it. By other boys.

And watching this group of boys not looking at the photo, you'd think that actually none of them really saw it. If we hadn't noticed one of them later, alone in the caff line, secretly looking again.

And if we hadn't noticed the subtle changes that day.

A boy stretching his arms down, trying to casually check his bicep.

A boy lifting his shirt to scratch his stomach but really checking his abs. Or lack thereof.

A boy buying a salad for lunch.

A boy swiping a ruler from maths so he could later try to calculate how he measured up.

A boy with no facial hair in Boots buying an electric razor to trim his pubes.

Miss is explaining this project we have to do next term. We've got to trace our own family history, and specifically our family's *female* history, whatever that means.

We're in period three and Slutty Scarlett actually has the nerve to come to class.

And two girls, neither of which are me I don't think, are doodling on the photo of Russell. One of them has a colour printer at home, so.

They're drawing a tattoo of their name on his appendage when Miss turns round and confiscates it. And I bet it's the first time she's ever seen one.

I bet it is. I bet she's still a virgin.

And before she even has time to ask it, one of the two girls, or someone else says:

'Scarlett sent it round.'

And Miss asks Scarlett if it's true. And one of the other girls starts to speak but Miss silences her – 'I'm asking Scarlett' – and I can't help but think of that scene from *The Crucible*, that's the school play this year, I'm playing John Proctor on account of there not being enough boys who auditioned, and there's that scene where I say: 'Tell the truth!' to my wife just like Miss is saying now and our not being condemned to death hangs on what comes out of her mouth.

Except this is nothing like that. Because Scarlett knows she's condemned no matter what she says. And so when Miss asks again: 'Did you send it, tell the truth,' she says:

'Sure.'

Sure. Not yes, not no, but…

And it's weird cos for a moment I think maybe she didn't – like if she'd protested her innocence I'd have thought for sure she's actually done it, liar, but her just...

Maybe she thinks in taking the blame she'll win favour with the girls.

Or maybe she knows the headteacher's office is safer than the corridors.

Or maybe she knows that it doesn't matter what she says or whether she did or not because it's already been decided.

Or maybe she thinks that this will end it. And the past two days will be a distant memory, forgotten.

And that's what I mean about Scarlett being dumber than she acts, bless her. I actually feel really bad. Because still, after all these years, she hasn't learned that St Helen's girls never forget. She thinks this is the end. But I know it's just the start. And there's nothing not one of us can do to stop it.

Change. Eleven years old.

I get my period. Thank fuck I'm not the last. So Sir says I don't have to go swimming. And I realise this will be a convenient excuse in future PE lessons.

We are all getting changed, nervous in our new school that has a swimming pool.

We are eleven years old. And though we are quiet pretending to concentrate on the arduous task of putting on swimsuits, we are really concentrating on taking casual glances at the others.

See who else has hair down there.

Who else doesn't really have boobs yet

Who is wearing a sports bra

Who is wearing no bra

Who is wearing a real bra.

No one. Except Scarlett.

And in the change-room after swim, she starts like putting on this lotion. Because her skin is dry she says. This lotion that smells like strawberries.

And this cherry-smelling Vaseline on her lips, because her lips are dry she says.

And it's like waving a steak rump around when my dog's wandered off. She'll walk down the corridor and the boys will come running.

Which is just the strangest thing, because this is Scarlett. Scarlett who wasn't even invited to all the parties, Scarlett who was last to get the accessory that everyone else already had, last to be picked.

And she has this confidence, this quiet confidence even when she's getting changed for swim. And it's like where did that come from? And she's suddenly started making these jokes. Like she's a comedian. I can't think of any, but yeah she makes these jokes.

And the boys always flock. Like bees to honey

Bees don't actually flock, they swarm

Sweating through their tight shirts

Nervously running hands through their faux-messy gelled coiffed hair

Annoyingly fingering the branded bands of their pants, cos all the boys were suddenly wearing boxers. And like branded ones

Stupidly laughing at her jokes

They're not even funny, not really

She has to barely utter two words and the boys start panting, wagging their tails.

Beat.

Maneater.

Beat.

The boys are disgusting anyway.

But really we get it. We get that it's not really about the boys for Scarlett. It's about attention. It's about for once not being at the bottom. Which is a bit pathetic really.

We take turns showing Sir our dives.

And Scarlett makes a big ugly splash on account of her boobs adding weight, serves her right.

Sir gives us five minutes' free time at the end and plays classical music over the speaker so we play calmly.

Someone gets the idea that we should pretend we're synchronised swimmers, which is dumb, but we do it anyway.

We lie on our backs in the water, a circle

My hands on her shoulder and her shoulder

Hers on her shoulder and her shoulder

Hers on her shoulder and her shoulder

Hers on her shoulder and her shoulder

And then we kick our legs up into the air.

It only lasts a moment before we all go underwater, the weight of someone's hands on our shoulders, drowning us

But for a moment it's the prettiest thing you ever saw.

Change. Present.

Last night my sister asked me why? 'Why did she take the photo?' Like I know.

But I did wonder about it. For a minute like. When I got the photo.

Probably it was a boy. Russell. Or. And probably he made her feel that if she didn't he'd lose interest. Cos some other girl would.

Probably he told her he'd be her boyfriend if she did.

Probably he threatened to tell everyone they slept together if she didn't.

Or. No. No.

Probably he made her feel special.

Probably he said it was just a bit of fun.

Probably he said: 'Show me yours I'll show you mine.'

Probably he made her feel pretty. Probably he made her feel like the most beautiful girl in the world.

Beat.

Or maybe he didn't.

Probably he made her feel ugly.

Probably he made her feel she could never get a guy like him.

Probably he made her feel worthless.

Probably he rejected her.

Probably he said he regretted what they'd done.

Probably she thought, if I just – flash, click, buzz –
then he'll… pay attention.

Beat.

Or maybe it wasn't a boy. Maybe she just took it. Just
to… see.

Maybe she wanted to know what she'd look like if she
were a page-three girl.

And maybe it was innocent and maybe she can't wait
to get home to delete the photo from her desktop to
make sure the same thing doesn't happen to her! I
mean. I don't know what I'm saying. Never mind.

And thank God my ex-boyfriend is a decent loyal guy.
That's all I'm saying.

My sister is asking again *why*. As though somehow this
matters, as though this changes things. She does not
understand that this question is miles away, is a
question from another dimension. And when I ignore
her, she asks: 'Why does a photo make someone a
slut?' But it's too complicated to explain, so I don't.

I'm thinking *why*. We're all wondering *why* when we
see Scarlett in the corridor after school. Why didn't she
just go home, leave school, leave the country, move to
Mozambique.

There she is in the corridor like always. As though
she's been asleep these past two days.

And I can feel it. My grandma, who had arthritis, used
to say she could feel when it was gonna rain. Feel it in
her bones. Well I can feel it, a storm's coming. And so
when Scarlett glances at me, I say – with my eyes, I
say, 'Run, run as fast as you can, get away from here'.
But she doesn't hear me, or chooses not to.

And I should probably leave. I should probably not be
here.

But then I'll miss something and tomorrow when everyone's –

'There's the ho.'

It's this girl I've never seen before. She doesn't go to our school I don't think.

And we find out later, that she text Scarlett while she was in the headteacher's office all afternoon. 'Meet me after school.' And like a moron, she comes.

Didn't her mother teach her anything?

Maybe she thinks she can explain.

Maybe she thinks at least a crowded corridor will keep her protected. What with students and teachers.

But the teachers have reports to write, and though their doors be open, they got invisible earplugs. They teach 'em how to do that in teacher training. And the students… well we're just kids.

'I hear you got with my man Russ. That true?'

And she looks to Russ. But he doesn't say anything.

'I said is that true bitch?'

And I wonder why he doesn't say anything.

And I wonder why if it's true, this girl isn't angry at *him*. Why she's not confronting *him*.

And I wonder what school she goes to.

And I didn't know Russell had a girlfriend.

'You a retarded mute or something? I'm gonna ask you one last time – and stop looking at my man. Did. You. Get. With. Him?'

We watch. Frozen.

And she says. Scarlett says:

'Sure.'

She could've just said no. She could've run away. But Scarlett's not as dumb as she seems. Because at long last she gets it. As she takes in the girls she went to school with in a circle around her, these girls she grew up with, she understands that this was all decided in nursery when we sat in a circle holding hands. She understands that it doesn't matter what she says. Which is why she:

'Sure.'

Pause.

There's a silence for what feels like for ever.

And I know a teacher will come and ruin it. Not let us see the ending. (*Pause.*) But no one comes. And then some guy's voice yells:

'Hit the slut already.'

A slap doesn't sound how you think it will. Not like in the movies. It's… louder.

And a punch sounds like… gardening. Like a spade tapping soil.

And a kick sounds like windscreen wipers when it's not raining.

And I want to click to another video, close the tab. But I can't.

And it's different than YouTube. Cos in person you can smell it. And I understand now when people talk about 'smelling the fear', because it actually does. Smells like salt. It smells like piss.

And you can taste the blood. Like when you breathe it tastes sour.

But suddenly Scarlett raises her arm, scratches the girl's face.

Scarlett's a nail-biter, so it doesn't really… but still.

And Scarlett's kicking in all directions, and her body's writhing on the ground, and she manages to get herself on top somehow, and she comes away with a chunk of the girl's hair in her hands.

Because this girl, us, have all underestimated Scarlett. Because Scarlett knows she has nothing to lose.

She slaps the girl back and then she like... pauses. Looks at me.

At me I think.

I think at me.

As if to say...

To say...

The girl seizes the opportunity to get back on top, and seeing her hair in Scarlett's hands, she goes... mental. Like proper mental.

And even Scarlett knows she's no match now. So she just covers her head with her hands.

And I worry this girl is gonna kill her. If she keeps on, then Scarlett might...

And why doesn't someone do something? Why won't someone do something?
Why won't Russell say something, stop this?!

Why doesn't he pull them apart?

Why doesn't he run and get a teacher?

Why does he just.
Stand there.

Pause.

The next week someone asks where Scarlett is?

Miss answers that she has transferred to another school.

Which means there's only nineteen St Helen's girls at the school now. Which is a bit of an awkward number. It's a prime number.

And it's only later that I realise Russell was the only boy there. And the guy who called out, who said 'hit the slut' was in fact a girl. It was one of us.

Music. 'Better Than Revenge' by Taylor Swift. Again the girls put on headphones, sing along and do a dance. This time the dance is led by a GIRL WITH FLOWERS IN HER HAIR.

The music suddenly stops. The GIRLS *face away with their headphones.*

GIRL WITH FLOWERS IN HER HAIR

'Were you going to tell me?' He's looking at me like *I've* shot Martin Luther King or something. Like *I've* shot Bobby Kennedy.

'I'm telling you now.'

We're sitting in a park, enjoying one of the few days of sunshine. It's August 1968, one of the worst summers on record.

'Besides there's nothing to tell.'

He stares at a group of people our age smoking in the distance. A girl dances, moving her lips to a song we can't hear. And as if she has whispered some answer to him, he: 'We can live with my parents.'

And I laugh. I can't help it. And I remember why I love him.

'Well do you have a better idea?'

When did we become so old? We're only sixteen but I feel a century. And I wonder what the next century will look like. I start thinking about the year 2000 and what a strange number that seems and I picture us in flying cars.

And he's still talking. I catch the end of his diatribe when he: 'We don't have a choice.'

And just like that I know that while I love him, we will not grow old together. We will not fly a car together into the next millennium. Because like that, the free-wheeling laissez-faire hippy eco-warrior I have fallen in love with has dropped his costume and become just another traditional boy.

'We have to accept the consequences.'

Last year when we met, at a rally, I fell in love with the way he'd have to fill silences. Could always talk. Now it's just annoying.

'Are you sure it's mine?'

I say nothing.

'It doesn't matter. I'll love it anyway. We'll live at my parents' and – '

'It doesn't matter.' Finally I speak. 'It doesn't matter because it doesn't exist.'

And he gives me this look. An ugly look. A look of disdain.

'Have you...?'

'Not yet.'

And he's relieved. His face loves me again.

And he starts talking again. But my mind is somewhere else. My mind is in some sci-fi future in the 2000s when my daughter and I fly our car to parliament where she is Prime Minister, a lady Prime Minister, when there is only love and not war. But even in the daydream I know that my daughter is not the same one, not this one inside me.

He's still talking about his parents' loft when I say: 'I'm sixteen.'

And before I can say more he's right in there as always – 'Sixteen's practically an adult. My parents were sixteen when they got married. We're capable of making mature decisions.'

And I agree. 'Which is why I can make this one. It's my body.'

And the look is back. He looks at me like I'm a...

And before he can say more, I'm up, I'm walking away from his voice in the park. And as I pass the other young people, the girl grabs my hand. She starts dancing with me. I don't hear any music – I'm fairly certain it's in her head, but I figure out the rhythm by copying her body. She leans in. For a second I think she's going to kiss me, but instead puts her mouth to my ear.

Whispers.

'Us girls need to stick together.'

She exits. The GIRLS *take off their headphones, turn back to face us.*

GIRLS   I stand in front of a full-length mirror.

My get-ready soundtrack.

She sings about how last Friday night we went skinny-dipping then had a *ménage à trois*.

She sings about how chains and whips excite me.

She sings about letting her see what you're hiding underneath, let her see your peacock, and it puts me in the mood.

I shave my pits

I wax my legs

I pluck my brows

I paint my nails

I colour my lips

I rose my cheeks

I darken my lashes

I straighten my hair

I lotion my stomach

I sparkle my arms

I dangle my ears

I spray my neck

I shave. Wax. Pluck. Paint. Colour. Rose. Darken.
Straighten. Lotion. Sparkle. Dangle. Spray. Wax.
Pluck. Paint. Colour. Rose. Darken. Straighten. Lotion.
Sparkle. Dangle. Spray. Wax. Pluck. Paint. Colour.
Rose. Darken. Straighten. Lotion. Sparkle. Dangle.
Spray. And take a photo.

Flash.

I hate the way I look

I hate how my ears stick out

I hate how small my lips are

I hate the little hairs above my lip

I hate the veins on my neck

I hate my stomach blubber

I hate my chunky arse

I hate my tiny breasts

I hate my wide hips

I hate my wrinkly knees

I hate my stubby hands

I hate my long feet

I take another photo. And it's time to go.

The party is at Tyler's house. He greets us in shorts, a
fur coat and no shirt. It's a 'pimps 'n' hos' party.

Rihanna plays and we love her.

Even though I've boycotted Rihanna on account of her
getting back together with Chris Brown, I make an
exception.

But that just shows what a strong woman Rihanna is. That she sticks by him despite what he did. That shows loyalty.

And we have a good time. I know this because people's Facebook statuses are updated to 'having a bare good time at Tyler's party'.

I know this because there are photos on Facebook showing us having a good time so we must be.

I know this because even though one of the girls is crying in a corner with mascara running down her face, we are still dancing and drinking.

And I hear Tyler tell one of the boys she's a cock-tease

Prude

Tight

Cold

Ice queen

Lead him on

Vamp

Prick-tease

Which is true. If you're gonna dress like that and then not, y'know?

And if you get a guy excited and then don't... like they can have problems, have to go to hospital, right?

What a bitch.

And I want to say, it's all bullshit. I want to say it doesn't make any sense. I want to ask about the space in-between. Cos she's a prick-tease cos she didn't, and she'd be a slut if she did, so how does she get to the space between? I want to be in the space between! I want to say this, but Rihanna is swirling through my brain, and alcohol is swirling through my veins or the other way round and I can't get the words to come out. And anyway, somewhere deep down I know the answer. In-between doesn't exist. So I just dance. And take a photo.

It is two in the morning and I could totally kill a Big Mac right now. Like a real one. Not Russell's.

We all could.

There's a good chance we won't notice. She's making a big effort to keep her head down, to be invisible. And through vodka-eyes focused on dipping fries into BBQ sauce there's a good chance no one will notice her.

Except someone, I don't think it's me, someone says: 'Look'. And the skulk of foxes raise their ketchup-blushed faces in unison.

It's been a good two months since we've seen her. I almost don't recognise her.

She's had a haircut, she's dyed her hair. And except for the tiny scar by her eyebrow, you wouldn't even know.

What she's doing at McDonald's with some guy in the middle of the night, I can't say.

Some guy from her new school.

And even when we were little we understood the rules always still applied – even out of school. Unless you ran into someone with their mum, and then it was smiles and a wave or small talk while your stupid mothers chatted to each other. But otherwise, the rules still applied, which is why –

'Scarlett.'

Someone says it quietly. She doesn't hear. Or pretends not to.

'Scarlett.'

And still she focuses her eyes hard on the guy, not blinking. Like maybe if she focuses hard enough we'll just disappear. Or maybe she will.

'Scarlett.'

You know the penis game we used to play in year nine? Like someone starts quietly then the next person says it a bit louder, then louder?

They get louder with each 'Scarlett'.

'Scarlett'

'Scarlett'

'Scarlett'

'Scarlett'

'Scarlett'

'Scarlett!'

Till even the fifty-year-old Ronald McDonald behind the counter is looking over at us. And more importantly the boy with Scarlett is looking over. And we're all barking:

'Scarlett! Scarlett! Scarlett!'

And it's funny. Cos I can't remember the last time I played a game.

And then someone goes over. Not me. I don't – I would never… I just watch.

'Scarlett, how are you?
Scarlett, don't you recognise me? Scarlett and I grew up together.'

Scarlett still just stares ahead. Like she's scared or something. Like she's mixed us up with the girl who came after school that day. Like in Scarlett's mind we're all the same person.

'Scarlett? Hello? Anyone in there?'

And I don't understand why she doesn't say something. Speak up! It is 2013! Women have earned the right to speak! She just keeps staring at the guy like she's a statue, still not blinking.

And I think maybe she's died. You hear about it.

But then some water starts to come out of one of her eyes so I know she's alive.

'Scarlett is an amazing photographer. Has she shown you any?'

But the girl can't find it on her phone. And Scarlett's eyes finally blink. A hint of relief. A different ending.

But then another girl, I, or whoever it is, says: 'I've got it.' And finds the boy's phone on her Bluetooth and presses send.

Buzz. Click.

And then we leave. Or else it'll be another thirty minutes for the next night bus.

Change. Twelve years old.

'Gimme Whatchya Got' by Chris Brown plays.

We are sat in a circle.

An empty Coca-Cola bottle spins fast.

We are twelve years old. We are sat in the loft of a boy called Tyler's house.

My mother has let me come because Tyler's parents will be there. Though you wouldn't know it. I have yet to see them. But when someone went to the loo downstairs she said she heard a loud TV so they probably are.

The bottle lands on one of us, and the girl who it lands on is nervous.

She's petrified. Scarlett.

But she doesn't show it. She acts like it's every day that she kisses Russell with the sweep-away hair. She doesn't let on that this will be the first time she has ever kissed a boy.

She doesn't let on that while she fancies Russell – everyone does – this wasn't how she'd pictured it in her head.

A room full of the girls she's grown up with and boys she doesn't really know chanting:

'Kiss kiss kiss tongue tongue tongue.'

She doesn't let on that it was supposed to be on their fifth date, it was supposed to be just the two of them, it was supposed to be with a rose in her hand, it was supposed to be like in the movies, it was supposed to be like how her mother told her.

And his tongue tastes of Doritos and Orange Fanta.

And when we've finished counting back from ten Russell says: 'Want to do it again?'

And she doesn't. Not really. But we're watching. And she knows we'll never forget if she doesn't. So she says:

'Sure.'

Beat.

Later we're sitting on couches and it feels like we're kids again or something because all the boys are on one couch and all the girls are on the other. And of course we can't all fit, so we sit on each other's knees

We sit on the floor leaning our heads on other girls' legs

We lie with our feet in other girls' laps.

And then Tyler brings out a laptop, hooks it up the TV. And says: 'Wanna see something?'

There are two men and one woman on the screen. All of them naked.

And at first I don't quite understand what I'm watching.

And I don't like it.

And I want to close my eyes.

And I want to say turn it off please.

And I want to get up and leave.

But she's sitting on my knee

And she has her head on my legs

And she has her feet in my lap

And I can't move.

So we sit there all of us and watch. Eating Doritos.

Change. Present.

If anything happens it will be his fault.

Yes, I blame the boy from McDonald's.

Why couldn't he have just kept it for himself?

Why couldn't he have just deleted it?

Why is it he felt so compelled to send it to others from his school?

What was it about the photo that offended him so?

It makes me really angry, the senseless things people do. His mother should have taught him better.

And if anything, if she like – then like it will be his fault. I hope he realises that. I hope he can like live with the consequences.

Scarlett is missing. She has been missing for over twenty-four hours. We know this because the police officer who comes to talk to our class tells us so.

He wants to know if any of us have heard from her.

'She doesn't go to this school any more,' I, or one of the other girls volunteer helpfully.

He's aware but thought perhaps some of us were still in touch with her. She was a St Helen's girl after all.

After all St Helen's girls are friends for life.

He thinks she may try to kill herself or have already done so. He doesn't say this in so many words.

He doesn't say this at all.

But we know. We are intelligent girls.

He also doesn't tell us that on the Monday after we saw her at McDonald's everyone at her new school had seen the photo. But we know this too. We have Twitter.

He also doesn't tell us that she left behind a note. We can't remember how we know this.

There is a girl in Canada who made a video before she killed herself.

Wait, is Canada in America?

And it's one of the first times a suicide was widely reported. Normally they don't cos they don't want it influencing impressionable young people.

In case we get ideas.

I mean how dumb is that? We're not so stupid that we're gonna kill ourselves just cos some girl on the news did.

The girl in Canada made this whole video, you can YouTube it, with cards and stuff talking about her naked photo that was sent around and her tormentors.

It's pretty grim. I thought Canadians were supposed to be nice. I'm not so sure any more.

At lunch, I decide to go for a walk

I decide to go home

I decide to eat by myself

I can't explain it, but I just. I don't want to see anyone. I don't want to see any of the girls.

And at night, the news is showing her school photo.

And I wish they'd stop showing it.

And the newsreaders keep asking – where did she go? Why did this happen? Who is responsible? When what they should really be asking is why isn't she smiling in the photo?

Why are her eyes in the school photo saying 'help me'?

And my mother says: 'Don't you know that girl?'

My mother says: 'Didn't that girl go to St Helen's?'

My mother says: 'Wasn't that girl at your birthday party once?'

My mother says: 'Wasn't that girl at our house once?'

My mother says: 'Didn't you have a sleepover with that girl one time?'

My mother says: 'Isn't that one of your friends?'

Yes

Yes

Yes

Yes

Yes

Yes.

And we take to Facebook and we write tributes:

'We miss you Scarlett. Come back.'

'We miss your beautiful smile.'

'We miss your winning personality.'

'We miss your jokes.'

'If you're reading this, know that – '

And some of us are on TV

The man is interviewing us

And we tell the camera:

'Scarlett was our friend. We miss her.'

'We miss her beautiful smile.'

'We miss her winning personality.'

'We miss her jokes.'

'If you're watching this Scarlett – '

And we cry. For real.

And I feel like I'm gonna throw up

And I feel like I've been punched in the stomach

And I feel like I've been kicked in the face

Because the screen switches to live footage. At the river. It's dark and you can't see anything. But the newsreader in the suit erases any doubt. They've found a body.

Music. 'Slut Like You' by P!nk. Again the GIRLS *put on headphones. This time the dance is led by a* GIRL WITH SHOULDER PADS.

But this time they can't quite get into it. Something is wrong. They don't really sing or do the dance with commitment. Some don't do it at all. Eventually they all stop, but before the music does. Beat.

Then the music suddenly stops. The GIRLS *face away with their headphones.*

GIRL WITH SHOULDER PADS

Olivia is singing let's get physical. When she kicks I kick, when she punches I punch. And the afternoon is replaying in my mind which only makes me kick higher and my forehead sweat harder and my heart pound faster. It is 1985 and soon girls will run the world. Just wait till I tell the girls at school.

I have only worked at Pierce, Richards and Stanley for a week. My mother is nervous. They don't normally take on girls as young as me, but I want to be a lawyer so my mum has made some calls and got me this after-school gig a couple hours a week. I am what you call a 'runner' at the law firm. And runner is not a euphemism. From four to six p.m. I run between floors delivering mail, delivering coffee, delivering photocopies, delivering staples and paperclips, delivering memos and faxes from other floors. Lucky for me Olivia has got me in shape, cos some of the other girls who are a bit – well they just can't work as fast as me. Which is why I don't think they like me very much. 'I'm raising expectations' one of them has told me. And we're supposed to stick together. But I can't help doing my job well, can I? I even bought a new outfit, just for work. *Work.* How cool am I? The girls are like what are you doing after school? 'Oh you know, I'm just going to work. To my law firm.'

And the girls tell me to stay out of Stanley's way. Stanley is his first name and his last name which is the dumbest thing I've ever heard. Unless the girls are just saying that to trick me, but I don't care. And then today I've got these papers I gotta deliver to Mr Stanley's secretary. Only she's on break so I knock on his door. The first thing he says is: 'That's a pretty outfit.' See, it's important to dress for success. That's what my mum says. I don't tell him this obviously. I just say: 'Thank you sir.' And this is where it gets really good. As I'm handing him his papers, he puts his hand on my waist and he says: 'What an efficient young woman you are. You'll be put to good use here.'

'I want to be a lawyer, sir.'

And his hand has subtly slid further down my waist.

'Well this will certainly be a good experience for you then,' he says.

'I thought so too,' I tell him. 'But I'm not so sure. See you're supposed to be this amazing lawyer, but you seem not to know about any kind of employment law.'

He doesn't understand.

'See this, right here, would be considered sexual harassment in the workplace. And you seem not to know that. Either that or you've assumed that because I'm wearing a pretty skirt that somehow means that's an invitation or I'm too young or naive to know otherwise. Either way, if you don't remove your hand from my firmly toned arse right now I will scream this whole office down, and then I will recruit Pierce, or Richards to sue the pants off you, and then I will call your wife.'

Beat.

'I'm glad you like my skirt. I'll be sure to wear it again.'

On my way out I see his secretary is back. She pretends to be typing on her Commodore 64 but I can see she's smiling.

When my mother picks me up, she asks how work was. I tell her 'fine' and she doesn't ask anything more. I turn up the car radio, Hall & Oates are singing:

She sings the last two lines of the third verse, and the first two lines of the chorus of 'Maneater' by Hall & Oates.

Here she comes indeed.

She exits. The GIRLS *take off their headphones, turn back to face us.*

GIRLS   The news doesn't show any photos, they're not allowed to. It might frighten us. We're only children after all.

Besides the family haven't identified the body yet.

There are counsellors in school in case any of us wants to talk. But the counsellors haven't got a clue.

We don't want to talk. What we want is to forget.

We are in history and we have brought candles. Miss has given us permission to put aside the presentations scheduled for today and instead do a kind of vigil.

And we stand in a circle holding candles, and we are each going to say a few words.

Except no one does. Not one says any words.

And Miss says: 'Would someone like to say something?'

Silence.

And then a girl's voice says

SCARLETT (*Appearing.*)
          I would like to say something.

GIRLS   And it's like a ghost. It's like we are nine years old with the Ouija board. Because standing there is Scarlett.

I can see her.

I can see her too.

And it's like, by being together, the St Helen's girls, we have brought forth the spirit of Scarlett into the room.

SCARLETT
          I would like to say something.

GIRLS   And it's like, it's almost like she's actually there...

Because she is actually there.

Beat.

At about this same moment, Scarlett's parents have confirmed the body from the river is not that of their daughter. Later discoveries will confirm the body is that of a fourteen-year-old Latvian prostitute and an autopsy will reveal she died with a boot to her skull.

SCARLETT

I have something to say.

GIRLS   And first I'm frightened, then I'm confused, then I'm relieved, then I'm actually angry. I feel like we've been duped.

We have been tricked.

We have shed tears, we have made tributes, we have lit candles, and for what?

SCARLETT

I would like to do my presentation now.

GIRLS   And Miss is so bewildered that all she can say is: 'Sure.'

SCARLETT (*Presentation notes in hand.*)

You have asked us to research the history of women in our family. Which was not especially easy as my mother is not a sentimental. No photos or nothing. But through a combination of some old shoeboxes of stuff at my nan's house, and newspapers and books found in the British Library in London where I have spent the last couple days FYI, I can tell you all the following:

My mother is one of only five female FTSE 100 chief executives. She did this, I imagine, by donning shoulder pads and body-checking any man who got in her way.

Her mother, my nan, was a teacher. Which doesn't tell me much about history. But when she was about my age, in the sixties, she marched with other women to make abortion legal. Which was like, a big deal. And she wore her hair in braids sometimes. And she had lots of sex. And no one judged her for it. Except maybe her mother. Were she alive. Because she, my great-grandmother, died when British European Airways flight 411 crashed on approach to Manchester from Amsterdam. This is ironic because from 1944 to '45 my grandmother worked as a pilot during the war delivering planes that needed to be fixed. Which, is like, not that an exciting job to have. She wasn't dropping bombs or anything. But it was a big deal, because she was doing a man's job. And men were bastards and didn't like girls like my great-grandma doing their jobs. And her mum... well she was a long time ago so I didn't find out much but her name's mentioned in an article in the *Daily Mail* from 1928 because she went to a scandalous pool party. I'm not sure why it was so scandalous. But the man who wrote it from the *Daily Mail* did not like that girls were dancing to Negro music and drinking cocktails in swimsuits. Which shows that some things don't change since the *Daily Mail* still does not like girls drinking and having fun but it does like photos of girls in swimsuits. So maybe things do change.

I have basically learned that in my family history there were always boys who were arseholes who made things shit for the girls in my family. But things have moved on for my generation. Because for me, it is not so much that boys are arseholes – they are – but more that the girls have become the arseholes the boys used to be. (*Puts away notes*.)

I used to ask myself every night *why*?

Why?

What did I ever do to you?

And then I would imagine twenty-five years from now coming to a school reunion and I'd be there in my Armani suit with my beautiful husband and my beautiful handbag and my beautiful children and when you all said: 'Scarlett! Scarlett!' I'd say: 'I'm sorry. I don't recognise you. I don't recognise any of you.' And then I'd leave.

But as I sat on the packed Tube in London, no one recognised me. No one pointed, no one whispered. And I realised you are all nothing. There is a big bad world out there where St Helen's means nothing. There is a big bad world that is just ready to swallow you up. But when it swallows up you lot, it will vomit you back up. Because you are indigestible girls. That's the kind of girls you are. You are food poisoning. And the world will know you are girls like that. And you will be all alone. Together, but alone. Do you see?

And I will forget you. I have forgotten you. Because I am not a St Helen's girl. But you will not forget me. After all, you have my photo to remember me by.

Exits.

GIRLS   A moment later we look around and realise we're still standing in a circle, holding lit candles.

Pause. No one knows what to do. Then they blow the candles out.

And the year is over. And now we must go our separate ways.

Well not me. Me and four of the girls are going to the same uni. We're going to be flatmates, which is like, it's gonna be totally… it's gonna be…

Oh God, what have I agreed to?

It's gonna be like actually amazing. We're gonna like see each other every morning when we wake up, when we go to bed.

Oh God.

It's the last day of school and so we run around signing messages on each other's school uniforms.

'Remember when'

'Remember when'

'Friends for ever'

'We'll always be'

I write 'We'll always be...' I'm meant to write 'friends', I'm meant to write 'Keep in touch'. But I... can't. Because I know it isn't true. Like these girls, running around with their marker pens are not, I suddenly realise... are not my friends. And suddenly I feel... so old. So very old. So I just leave it: 'We'll always be.'

I don't go. For the whole last week since Scarlett – I haven't gone in. I have a restlessness in my stomach like I'm pregnant. Which I'm not. Which is impossible. It is not the immaculate conception. Unless it is. Unless I am being punished. Maybe she has put a curse on me.

I write these emails where I – I don't actually send them to her. But I. I write them. And it makes me feel better. I am not a bad person. I am not Osama bin Laden or Simon Cowell. I am just... a girl.

I have decided to move to Canada. My mother has gone apeshit, thinks I've totally lost it. Not even like city Canada. Like proper Canada. Like I'm going to go live on a reserve with the indigenous people and go ice-fishing and there's no internet and no phone reception and I'm going to live in an igloo. 'What will you do for money?' my mother wants to know. I won't need money though because I'll trade in furs and I'll hunt for my food. It's just something I need to do.

I've accidentally been assigned a flat with all boys instead of girls for September. I explained to Mum that I called and it's too late and there's nothing they can do. So I can't change. But I never actually called.

I start crying. Out of nowhere just. And I don't know why. Maybe I'm just sad to be leaving all the girls.

I start a Facebook group. For the St Helen's girls. No one else is allowed. So that we can stay in touch.

I lift up my shirt and take a photo of myself in the mirror. I don't know why. I just do it. And then delete it.

I commit suicide.
Oh sorry not, not like for real. I mean Facebook suicide. I delete my account, my photos. Everything.

One of my hens is dead. Fox got her. And it's weird cos she was like Mother Hen, the one in charge. But the fox obviously didn't give a toss about the pecking order. Which kind of just defeats the whole purpose, doesn't it?

Something has changed. I'm looking at the signatures on my shirt to figure out who still needs to sign and it's like I recognise the names, but I don't know them. Does that make sense? And when did everything change? I try to rewind, to find and replay that moment when it changed... but I don't know when it was. When it was that I decided I no longer want to hang around girls like that. I can't find it. The video has been deleted, or violated the user agreement. It doesn't exist.

And I want to take a photo. A group photo.

Oh yes, one final photo of us all together!

Gather round!

But we're suddenly temporarily distracted by a group of boys who go running across the field in their pants.

There is no logic to why they do this. To why a group of boys are laughing, screaming, jumping on each other in their underwear.

Us girls sign school shirts. The boys run around half-naked. It's in our DNA somewhere.

And it confirms for me what Miss left out in history lessons. That while girls have got more intelligent over generations, boys have become more stupid.

And I'm a bit jealous. I want to run around in my pants instead of standing here with a marker pen. I imagine doing it. Just do it. Right now. Strip off, run over and join the boys.
But they're too far. They're gone. And I've missed my chance.

A photo! Gather round!

The St Helen's girls.

My mother told me these girls are my friends for life.

One final photo. To use for the Facebook page.

A photo with smiles, and her arm round her waist

And her arm round her waist

And her arm round her waist

And her –

But someone is not here today with stomach cramps

And someone is walking away to the toilets

And someone says it's a stupid idea

And someone says she doesn't want to be in the photo, she'll take it

Which defeats the purpose because it has to be all of us

And someone says: 'Well it's not going to be all of us anyway.' And I don't know what she means by that.

Like if she means it's my fault somehow. Like what does she mean by that?

Like would it kill her to be in a photo?

And those of us who are standing there with our arms round someone's waist just start looking kinda dumb, cos no one's taking the photo

So she takes her arm off her waist

And she takes her arm off her waist

And she

And the moment is gone, and there will not be a photo, which is actually really frustrating because we will look back on this moment and we won't remember it because we will not have a photo. And that's just a wasted opportunity, really

And I don't get why some of the girls have to spoil it for the rest of us

Why they can't just go along

Be a team player

There's always a couple who have to stand apart from the crowd just to prove a point. To feel individual. Which is pretty pathetic if you ask me

Girls like that ruin it for everyone

Bitches.

Sluts.

And so I just start snapping photos.

Flash

Flash

Flash.

But then

Crack.

Smash.

It falls.

It breaks.

Which is called pathetic fallacy. Or foreshadow. Or something. I dunno. All I know is I will never be with all the girls together again.

Change. Forty-five years old.

I am with all the girls together again.

We are in the dining hall.

Twenty five-year-olds are singing 'sleigh bells ring are you listening?'

We are forty-five years old. We are at St Helen's. They are tearing down the school, building a fresh new state-of-the-art all the bells and whistles blah blah.

And so all the former St Helen's girls are invited to come for a reunion of sorts.

There is about two hundred in all. Everyone from our year has made an appearance. And it's nice to see the old faces. Because over the years, despite our best intentions – well life gets in the way doesn't it.

And I'm not sure why I've come.

I can't believe I've come.

Maybe out of curiosity.

Maybe out of some weird twisted obligation.

Maybe I think I'm going to give her all the unsent emails I've written over the years.

Maybe to see her entrance. Like she promised.

And after the current reception class finishes singing we have some time to catch up. To reminisce about school shows when I was the lead.

And that boy we used to fancy... um Robert? Roger? Can't remember but one of the girls ran in to him and apparently he's fat and bald and works in IT.

And someone still sees Tyler, who used to have the parties, who has a much younger boyfriend who is a model. Go figure.

And it's like no time has passed at all. It's like we are sixteen again. Except that I *have* a sixteen-year-old. A daughter.

My daughter's ten.

Mine are six and eight.

Mine are twelve and thirteen, God help me. Can I fast-forward please?

My three are all boys. I still don't know what to do with them.

I had my tubes tied.

My girls are at the age where I say: how was school? And all I get is 'fine'. I've stopped trying to get more out of them. Futile.

And I look around for her. But she's not there. I don't think so anyway.

And as we're heading to the car park, I see the reception girls in the playground. But something's wrong.

One of them has built a snowman, but someone is trying to destroy it. A boy.

And I wonder if I should intervene. Should say something. But what would I say?

So we just watch.

And then suddenly without planning, without saying a word, the girls start to link arms. All twenty of them.

Making a barrier between the boy and the snowman.

Her arm in her arm

Her arm in her arm

Her arm in her arm

Her arm in her arm

Her arm in her arm

Her arm in her arm

Her arm in her arm

Her arm in her arm

Her arm in her arm

Her arm in her arm

Her arm in her arm

Her arm in her arm

Her arm in her arm

Her arm in her arm

Her arm in her arm

Her arm in her arm

Her arm in her arm

Her arm in her arm

Her arm in her arm

The GIRLS *stand at the front of the stage like at the start, facing the audience in a line – their arms linked.*

And then one of them speaks, the smallest of the group:

'Us girls stick together.
Think you can break through us, boy?
Go on. Just you try.'

End.

Other Plays for Young People to Perform from Nick Hern Books

Original Plays

100
Christopher Heimann,
Neil Monaghan, Diene Petterle

BANANA BOYS
Evan Placey

BLOOD AND ICE
Liz Lochhead

BOYS
Ella Hickson

BUNNY
Jack Thorne

BURYING YOUR BROTHER IN THE
  PAVEMENT
Jack Thorne

CHRISTMAS IS MILES AWAY
Chloë Moss

COCKROACH
Sam Holcroft

DISCO PIGS
Enda Walsh

EIGHT
Ella Hickson

HOLLOWAY JONES
Evan Placey

HOW TO DISAPPEAR COMPLETELY
  AND NEVER BE FOUND
Fin Kennedy

I CAUGHT CRABS IN WALBERSWICK
Joel Horwood

MOGADISHU
Vivienne Franzmann

MOTH
Declan Greene

THE MYSTAE
Nick Whitby

OVERSPILL
Ali Taylor

PRONOUN
Evan Placey

SAME
Deborah Bruce

THERE IS A WAR
Tom Basden

THE URBAN GIRL'S GUIDE TO
  CAMPING AND OTHER PLAYS
Fin Kennedy

THE WARDROBE
Sam Holcroft

Adaptations

ANIMAL FARM
Ian Wooldridge
Adapted from George Orwell

ARABIAN NIGHTS
Dominic Cooke

BEAUTY AND THE BEAST
Laurence Boswell

CORAM BOY
Helen Edmundson
Adapted from Jamila Gavin

DAVID COPPERFIELD
Alastair Cording
Adapted from Charles Dickens

GREAT EXPECTATIONS
Nick Ormerod and Declan Donnellan
Adapted from Charles Dickens

HIS DARK MATERIALS
Nicholas Wright
Adapted from Philip Pullman

THE JUNGLE BOOK
Stuart Paterson
Adapted from Rudyard Kipling

KENSUKE'S KINGDOM
Stuart Paterson
Adapted from Michael Morpurgo

KES
Lawrence Till
Adapted from Barry Hines

NOUGHTS & CROSSES
Dominic Cooke
Adapted from Malorie Blackman

THE RAILWAY CHILDREN
Mike Kenny
Adapted from E. Nesbit

SWALLOWS AND AMAZONS
Helen Edmundson and Neil Hannon
Adapted from Arthur Ransome

TO SIR, WITH LOVE
Ayub Khan-Din
Adapted from E.R Braithwaite

TREASURE ISLAND
Stuart Paterson
Adapted from Robert Louis Stevenson

WENDY & PETER PAN
Ella Hickson
Adapted from J.M. Barrie

THE WOLVES OF WILLOUGHBY
  CHASE
Russ Tunney
Adapted from Joan Aiken

For more information on plays to perform visit
www.nickhernbooks.co.uk/plays-to-perform

www.nickhernbooks.co.uk

 facebook.com/nickhernbooks

twitter.com/nickhernbooks